Contents

Introduction

For some people, film is an art, like painting, music or poetry. For others, it is just an industry which makes and sells products – just as a food company might make and sell baked beans.

This book is about the ways the film industry makes, distributes and shows films. The book concentrates on **feature films**. Feature films are full-length (at least 72 minutes long) narrative, or story, films made on **celluloid** (not video) and made to be shown in cinemas. Because the film industry is genuinely international, this book does not limit itself to the workings of the British film industry.

How to write a hit movie

Someone, somewhere, must once have written a movie script, sent it to a film studio, and had it immediately accepted and made into a film. That's not how it usually works.

A film may come into being because someone with plenty of money has seen a play or read a book that would make a good film – and then buys up all the rights to make a film of that 'property'. He or she may or may not get round to actually doing it – but as long as they hold the rights, no-one else can make the film. Not even the original author of the book.

A film may also be made because a **director** and a star decide they would like to work together. 'Yeah, especially if it's in Africa. Or the Caribbean...' So they must create a story with a good role for the star, set in a country that looks like the one of their choice.

Within days of the tragic death of Princess Diana, people in the film industry were talking about making a film about her life and death. One agency had soon signed up fifteen look-alike actresses and six possible scripts. An American **producer** wondered if an English accent was a turn-off. Another producer thought it would make a good television movie, but was not suitable for the cinema due to its 'non-positive ending factor' (i.e. the heroine gets killed).

Concept

The idea for a film is often called the concept. It may come from a writer, producer or director. In its first stage, the concept will be written down very briefly. A possible concept for an original film is shown opposite.

Outline

Next, the producer will require an outline. This is a more detailed description of the plot or storyline, the main characters, locations and settings. The outline will normally be less than 500 words long, but it may take two or three drafts before it is accepted.

Treatment

The next step is writing the **treatment**. To do this, the producer hires a writer (who may or may not see the film through to its conclusion).

The treatment is a summary of the way the writer will treat the proposed story. It includes descriptions of atmosphere and mood, details about the major characters and actions, and suggestions for locations and character development.

> MERCENARY
>
> 1. This will be a film about mercenary soldiers, showing how they become victims rather than profiteers of war.
>
> 2. A young man, unable to find work in Britain, is attracted through the Internet to join a shady organization offering the chance of wealth and adventure in an African war.
>
> 3. The man joins up, but his assignment (laying illegal landmines), and the reality of war in a poverty-stricken country, lead him to attempt to escape the organization, and to publicize its desire to prolong the war.

An example of a concept for a film.

MEDIA F⊙CUS

Film

David Self

Heinemann
LIBRARY

First published in Great Britain by Heinemann Library
Halley Court, Jordan Hill, Oxford OX2 8EJ
a division of Reed Educational and Professional Publishing Ltd.
Heinemann is a registered trademark of Reed Educational & Professional Publishing Limited.

OXFORD MELBOURNE AUCKLAND
KAMPALA JOHANNESBURG BLANTYRE GABORONE
IBADAN PORTSMOUTH (NH) USA CHICAGO

Designed by Jim Evoy
Illustrations by Jeff Edwards
Printed in Hong Kong

03 02 01 00 99
10 9 8 7 6 5 4 3 2 1

ISBN 0 431 08251 0

This book is also available in a library hardback edition (ISBN 0 431 08246 4).

Self, David
    Film. – (Media focus)
    1. Motion picture industry – Juvenile literature
    I. Title
    302.2'343

Acknowledgements

The Publishers would like to thank the following for permission to reproduce photographs:
All Action/Ellis O'Brien, p. 7; Aquarius Library, p. 27; BFI Stills, Posters & Designs, pp. 14 (left), 17
(bottom), 24, 28; Canal/National Film Archive, p. 18; Channel Four Stills Dept, p. 19; Columbia
Pictures, p. 22; Kobal Collection, pp. 5 (top), 12 (left), 17 (top); Moviestore Collection, pp. 10, 14
(right), 16; Popperfoto, p. 23; Ronald Grant Archive, pp. 9, 20, 21; Smith, John, p. 9 (bottom);
Telegraph Colour Library, p. 5 (bottom); United Cinemas International, p. 25; Worsfold, Mel,
p. 12 (right).

Cover photograph reproduced with permission of Tony Stone Images Ltd.

Our thanks to Steve Beckingham, Head of Media Studies, Fakenham College, Norfolk, and to
Kingsley Canham, Programme Director, Cinema City, Norwich for their comments in the
preparation of this book.

Every effort has been made to contact copyright holders of any material reproduced in this book.
Any omissions will be rectified in subsequent printings if notice is given to the Publisher.

Any words appearing in the text in bold, **like this**, are explained in the Glossary.

Choices made by the writer can have a huge effect on the cost of filming. For example, a crowd or battle scene may involve thousands of extras and an enormous **set**.

A treatment for *Mercenary* might begin: *It is a hot, sultry evening in north London. The camera zooms in on a run-down street. Two small boys are playing a war game on the derelict wreck of a burned-out car...*

Screenplay

If the producer approves the treatment and has begun to put a deal together (see page 6), the writer starts work on the first draft of the screenplay. The first draft separates the scenes and includes at least some of the dialogue and action, as well as more general acting and technical directions. From this point on, the screenplay is revised several times with the help of the director and producer.

Other writers may be called in to help with various parts of the script. At one time, each of Hollywood's film **studios** had its own stable of writers, with individuals specializing in certain types of scene. For example, one writer would work on the dialogue, another would write the jokes, and another would script the fights.

Not all films are written in this way, though. A number of major directors have insisted on writing their own scripts, either alone or with one trusted writer to help them.

'The best filmwriting ... doesn't tell the director, the actors or the cameraman what to do. A screenplay should stand or fall by a bare description of what is happening and what is said. A screenplay is about writing as little as possible.'
John Hodge, one of the creators of *Trainspotting*.

Film

The earliest still photographs were made on glass plates. But in order for cinematic photography (that is, moving pictures) to work, photographs had to be captured on a transparent substance, like glass, but which could bend easily. Cinematic photography became possible with the invention of **celluloid**.

Celluloid is thin, transparent and flexible. It usually consists of a base of cellulose acetate coated with light-sensitive emulsion and other chemical salts. When the emulsion is exposed to light through a camera's **lens**, the salts alter to form an image, which can be seen once the film has been developed.

Since 1900, the standard size of film for professional filmmaking has been 35mm wide. Each **frame** has four perforations on either side, which allow the reel of film to be moved and positioned.

35mm film like this is used to make the majority of feature films today.

Pre-production

There are as many ways of making a film as there are films. What they all need is money. Finding the money is the producer's job.

Although the **producer** has to find the money for a film, he or she no longer simply hands the project over to creative people like the **director**. Today, most producers want to keep some kind of control over their property. As the producer David Puttnam once said, 'I don't want to be a banker to someone else's ideas... I need a sense of ownership, which I can only get from developing my own material.'

As we have seen, the first stage for the producer is finding a concept, developing an outline from it, and commissioning a **treatment**. Alongside this, the producer must set about persuading other people to get involved in raising development money. This is the money that is needed to pay the writer, and to pay all the expenses involved in putting the whole package together.

The package

The package is designed to attract investors to promise the money that will pay for the production of the film itself. The package consists of the concept and outline, the names of the director and the stars, and an outline of the budget (how the money will be spent). With this package, the producer can approach various people to ask them to fund, or 'bankroll', the film.

In a few cases, the money may come from just one source. A 1995 British film, *The Madness of King George* (costing £8 million), was financed almost entirely by the American Samuel Goldwyn Company, although the television station Channel 4 did provide some

money. More often than not, however, the producer must approach a large number of companies and other organizations. In Britain, these might include:
- rich private investors
- television companies
- satellite TV stations (who will want the right to show the film on their movie channels)
- film distribution companies (who promise to provide the money once the film is completed – banks then advance a loan against this promise)
- government sources (for example, British Screen Finance Ltd)
- American investors
- the National Lottery.

Most investors will not only want their money back; they will want a share of the profits as well. In order to make a profit for everyone involved, a film usually has to earn 2.5 times what it costs to make.

Collecting all the funding so that the film can go ahead is called 'putting together a deal'. It can take many years. Often, packages unravel and concepts and dreams go up in smoke. Occasionally, a deal is struck.

Executives and associates

'Executive producer' is a title often given to the person who provides most of the money, while 'associate producer' may be anyone who has done anything useful such as finding one of the sources of the money, or even providing the concept for the film.

Development

Once a deal with the investors has been made, the producer begins employing staff (including the director) and setting the production process in motion. From now on, the producer controls budgets, schedules, publicity and all other business matters.

Filming is expensive – especially location work – and it must be carefully planned to make sure it is as economical as possible. Travel needs to be kept to a minimum, which will almost certainly mean working on scenes out of their natural order. A whole variety of factors must be taken into account when choosing locations. For example, will it be cheaper to pay everyone to do nothing while waiting for a sunny day on a Cornish beach, or take everyone to the Sahara? Is there a suitable hotel at which the cast and crew can stay? Is there an indoor location nearby which can be used for indoor scenes, when bad weather prevents use of the outdoor location? Have the owners of the property (or the police or local authority) given permission for filming?

The producer must keep a very tight control on two categories of spending:

• above-the-line costs – expenses agreed upon before the shooting of a film, including the purchase of the property, or story, and salaries for such people as the screenwriter, producer, director and performers.

• below-the-line costs – expenses that arise after filming begins – for example, expenses for shooting, **editing**, and all production business.

Stars mean box-office success

In July 1995, it was announced that Mel Gibson would get $25 million for the film *Ransom*. That meant he would get $20 million up-front (at the start of filming), and the rest would come as back-end participation – a percentage share of what the film would make at the box office. By now, he could have earned very much more than $25 million (about £17m).

Why do producers pay this sort of money? Because star names mean box-office success. All the evidence shows that a star's name attached to a film helps to make it a success when it opens.

The cost of a film

Film budgets are closely guarded secrets. When talking to the press about budgets, producers often either increase them to make the film sound more lavish than it is, or understate them in order to make the producer seem clever with money.

Arnold Schwarzenegger attending the movie première of Eraser.

APPROXIMATE BUDGETS OF SOME FILMS MADE IN 1996:

BRITISH FILMS:

FEVER PITCH	£1.75M
THE FULL MONTY	£1.60M

BRITISH CO-PRODUCTIONS:

BEAN	£16.2M
WILDE	£6.4M

In production

Producers aren't fat guys with big cigars who sit around all day doing nothing. They work. Mind you, they do have plenty of assistants.

Once there is enough money to make the film, the **producer** and the **director** can think about supervising the writing of the screenplay by the screenwriter.

At the same time, the producer has to set up the production team, select locations and **studios**, and work out a production schedule.

Scheduling

On a good day, a film crew might manage to shoot three minutes of usable film. A full-length **feature film** can therefore easily take seven weeks to shoot, and more if there are complicated scenes. The shoot needs careful planning if it is to be done as economically (i.e. cheaply) as possible. All sorts of matters have to be taken into account. Because of these, a film is rarely shot in anything like the order in which we see it. Some of the basic facts a producer must bear in mind when planning a production schedule include:
• it is expensive to return to a location more than once. Shoot all you have to in one place before moving everyone on
• shoot **exterior** shots as soon as the weather permits
• child actors need chaperones (guardians) and are allowed to work only a certain number of hours per day
• it can take a long time to alter a location for a period shot – for example, hiding yellow lines on roads, temporarily repainting shop fronts, and erecting old fashioned street lights

• stunts always take a long time to prepare
• actors may have other commitments and may not be available every day
• you must limit the length of time you hire special equipment, such as classic cars.

Members of the crew

Besides the producer, director, writer, and executive and associate producers, the following people will become involved at this stage:
• The art director or production designer is responsible for the look of everything that appears on screen. This means (a) designing and overseeing the construction of studio settings, and (b) helping to select and adapt locations outside the studio.
• The costume designer works with the art director to ensure that all the costumes (whether they are modern or historical) fit properly into the overall design of the film.
• The construction manager supervises the actual building of the sets.
• The casting director suggests actors to play any characters in the film who have not yet been cast. He or she is often involved in negotiating how much each actor gets paid.
• The **unit** production manager organizes transport, accommodation, meals, etc., and also prepares a file of useful information. This includes maps, addresses, phone numbers, train times, schedules of each day's shooting (**call sheets**), and details of where costumes, props and people need to be each day – even where cars should or should not be parked.

Production values

The term 'production values' refers to the quality of the look and sound of a film: its sets, costumes, properties, lighting, colour, camera technique, music and dialogue. High production values make a film pleasurable and satisfying to watch and hear.

The film company MGM was known for the high production values of many of its films from the mid-1930s to the mid-40s, including The Wizard of Oz *(1939) which cost the then amazing amount of $3.7million.*

Location finding

Locations, along with casting, can have a major effect on a film. Producers often employ location managers, whose job is to find suitable locations for particular films. A building called Bush House in London has been the Kremlin in Moscow; Greenwich gasworks in London was a Japanese shipworks in *Empire of the Sun*. The real setting is often unusable because it is too far away or because it is impossible to film there. Baker Street in London is too busy to be closed off for days while a Sherlock Holmes film is made – but Cowley Street in Westminster looks just like it. To make it look old-fashioned, film-makers change the street signs and fill it with horse-drawn carriages.

Producers need permission from many different authorities (such as the local council, police force or fire brigade) before filming can happen in any public place. After all, a film crew may consist of 50 people and 30 or more vans, caravans and trucks. They cannot just park anywhere.

UK production facilities

The United Kingdom has several major film studios capable of housing the biggest productions, especially at Pinewood and Shepperton. With the recent growth of the British film industry, two new studios opened – one at Radlett, where the Bond film *Tomorrow Never Dies* was made, and another at Leavesden, used for the latest *Star Wars* films. Both are in Hertfordshire, north of London.

Britain is home to some of the best special-effects companies and digital-effects companies in the world. It is also popular with film-makers because different types of scenery (such as mountains, forests, coastlines, cities and old-fashioned villages) can be found in a relatively small area – which cuts down travelling time and costs.

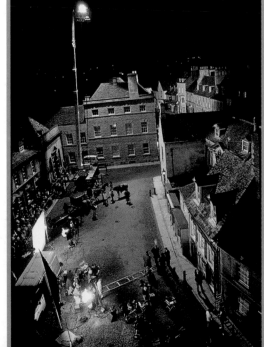

Filming BBC TV's Middlemarch *on location in Stamford, Lincolnshire.*

The shoot

The procedure is remarkably simple. First you film one shot. Then you film the next. And so on, through the day.

In practice, it's more complicated. The design department begins by preparing the **set**. Lighting is set up. The camera is put in place. Dressers help actors to dress, and make-up artists do everything from helping the leading man to stop sweating to creating scars, beards or werewolves. The dialogue coach helps the stars get their lines right. Then the scene is rehearsed and everyone waits for the sun to reappear, before the scene is filmed.

Naturally it takes even longer. Scenes often have to be relit, or shot again because something was not exactly right. Each **take** is numbered (for example Shot 3, Take 11), and the take number is shown on the clapperboard that is filmed at the beginning of each take (see page 12). By the end of the day, a vast number of shots and a few minutes of usable film will be '**in the can**'.

The **director** is helped by the **first assistant director**, who summons the various actors onto the set at the right time, directs **extras** and tries to keep everyone happy. There may be a second assistant director, who liaises with the **producer**, and even a third assistant who helps the first assistant director.

Lighting

It is not enough for a scene to be visible. It must be bright enough for the camera to see. Simply shining one light at an object may make it clear, but it can also deprive it of depth or solidity; so lighting must be used to maintain its three-dimensional qualities. A second purpose of lighting is to highlight appropriate characteristics and conceal or hide others. It can also suggest a mood or atmosphere.

The director of photography is responsible for lighting the set or location, and for the general composition of the scene, the colours of the images, and the choice of cameras, as well as **lenses**, filters, and **film stock**, and all the camera settings and movements. He or she controls both technical and artistic quality.

On outdoor locations, available light (daylight) may seem the sensible choice. Nature often needs some artificial help, however, because:
• strong sunlight can create unwelcome contrasts and areas of deep shadow
• the director may want to film a scene in the late afternoon in a setting which is by then in shadow
• cloud can result in dull, boring pictures
• it may be a day of constantly changing light conditions, in which no two shots would match without the use of artificial lighting.

When filming on location, the camera may be mounted on tracks so it can be moved smoothly.

Small battery-powered lamps are often sufficient to light close-ups and small scenes, but larger areas require high-intensity lamps powered by a generator or mains supply.

With **interior** locations, existing lighting is almost invariably too weak or wrongly positioned, usually being too high and so lighting only the tops of the actors' heads. The director of photography must know before setting out for the location what the director will be content with. Will it be just a few intimate settings in nooks and crannies of an ancient castle (which is easy)? Or will the audience have to see every corner of a banqueting-hall (expensive)?

Specialist services

A wide range of back-up services become involved in location work. Besides obvious ones (such as lighting hire companies), there are firms that specialize in providing all kinds of services, people and props. These might include performing animals (with handlers and trainers), stunt men and women, underwater and aerial photography, hot-air balloons, underwater explosions, artificial snow-making machines, and transport for film, equipment, crews and cast.

There are also specialized location caterers, who can provide not only coffee and rolls, but full-scale meals suitable for stars and even gourmet technicians. Neither group is usually happy to settle for a sandwich, even halfway up Ben Nevis.

Continuity

The continuity girl (also known as the continuity clerk, script clerk or script girl) keeps a record of the number and duration of each **take**, the direction of movement, characters' positions, costumes, props, and furniture. This ensures that the next shot will match exactly, even if it has to be filmed some time later. This job is unusual in the still shamefully male-dominated film industry, because it is almost always done by a woman.

How a film camera works

The camera photographs a series of images, normally at the rate of 24 **frames** per second. The container in which the film is loaded before it is attached to the camera is called the cartridge or magazine.

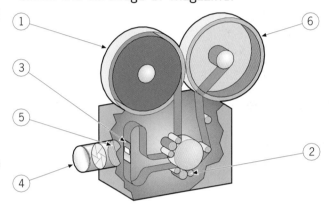

The film travels downwards from the feed, or full spool (1), moved by the sprocket wheels (2), whose teeth fit into the perforations or holes in the film. It stops for a brief moment in the 'gate' (3) behind the lens (4). The lens **focuses** the light rays coming in from the scene outside into a clear image. Between each picture, the shutter (5) whirls round to cut off the light rays before the film travels downwards. Then the film moves up to the take-up spool (6).

When the film has finished this journey through the camera, it travels in a light-tight cartridge or can to the laboratory to be developed.

Film sound

The sound for the film is recorded separately, and matched to the camera **footage** at the **editing** stage (see pages 12–13).

Post-production

Actors will always tell you their best scenes end up on the cutting-room floor. Film editors know otherwise.

Post-production refers to all the stages the various pieces of film and soundtrack must go through before they become a completed film, ready for showing.

The main job is **editing**. Put in its simplest terms, this means selecting the best **takes** and assembling them into what should be their final order in the film. Cutting is sometimes used as another word for editing (hence the name **cutting room**), but it does not properly describe the many skills required to make the film tell its story effectively.

A Steenbeck editing table, a well-known piece of editing equipment.

The editor's first task is to match up the images and the sound. At the start of each shot, when the two pieces of the clapperboard visibly come together, they make a clapping sound, which appears on the separately recorded soundtrack. By lining up the two, the editor can make sure sound and vision will be 'in sync' (that is, together) for the rest of the shot.

The editor works at a flatbed editing table. The film and soundtracks run horizontally across the table and the picture is projected onto a small screen. Several takes of the same scene can be run at once, so the editor can switch between them, selecting the best bits. It is also possible to build up cross-cutting sequences, which intersperse images from two or more different scenes.

Gradually, the editor makes the first, 'rough' cut of the film. It will follow the storyline, but without any fine or detailed editing. This cut is also frequently called the director's cut, because it is largely the way the **director** sees the film, without any interference from the **producer** or film **studio**.

The director and editor may work through the film many more times and there will be several more intermediate cuts. At last, the editor makes the fine cut, which includes the final arrangements of shots and sequences, each cut to exactly the right length. The fine cut includes effects such as fades and **dissolves**, as well as any special-effects photography. This version may contain only one-tenth of the film originally shot: the rest has been cut out. The fine cut also includes the **credits** and titles.

The stages of post-production

The soundtrack

A good proportion of the sound we hear on a film is not recorded on location. For all kinds of reasons, the 'real' sound may be muffled, faint or otherwise unusable. When this happens, the actors (or 'sound-alike' actors with similar voices) have to **post-sync** the dialogue. This means re-recording the lines to match the movements of the actors' lips on the screen.

The various soundtracks, including original location recordings, post-sync dialogue and special sound effects, are then mixed by the **dubbing** editor. Along with music, they form the soundtrack of the film. In a film called *Duet for One*, a simple scene involving a bus ride through a city centre needed ten separate tracks of sound effects, including traffic, conversation inside the bus, a large fountain, and 'atmos', (short for atmosphere, which means low level, background noise). A large-scale battle scene can easily demand 150 tracks.

The editor works very closely with the dubbing mixer, supervising the final blending of all the soundtracks into a master track. Eventually the fine cut is matched with the final sound mix, and the two are sent to a laboratory where they are printed together on the answer print, sometimes known as the composite print or trail composite. All the release prints (copies of the film to be shown in cinemas) are made from the answer print.

Credits

As well as the name of the film, the front credits (shown at the beginning) normally include the distribution company, the production company, and the star performers. The front credits usually conclude with the producer's and director's names, for example: 'A Robert Altman Film'.

End titles, or closing credits, usually list all the actors and their roles, together with all the technical and production staff who have worked on the film.

The way stars and other contributors are billed in a film matters very much to them, because it's a way of telling the film industry how important they are in that film – and how much they deserve to be paid in their next one!

•DID YOU KNOW?•DID YOU KNOW?•DID

Film music

BACKGROUND MUSIC – MUSIC THAT ACCOMPANIES THE ACTION OF THE FILM BUT COMES FROM NO SOURCE WITHIN THE FILM. OFTEN USED TO HEIGHTEN THE MOOD OF A SCENE.

SOURCE MUSIC – MUSIC THAT COMES FROM A SOURCE WE CAN SEE ON THE SCREEN, SUCH AS A BAND PLAYING.

ORIGINAL SCORE – MUSIC SPECIALLY WRITTEN FOR A PARTICULAR FILM.

CANNED MUSIC – MUSIC THAT HAS ALREADY BEEN COMPOSED, RECORDED AND (OFTEN) PUBLISHED, AND WHICH IS RE-USED IN A FILM.

DID YOU KNOW?•DID YOU KNOW?•DID

Rushes viewed daily

Promotional campaign begins

Editing begins

Marketing plans developed

Principal photography completed

Special effects completed

Director's cut produced

Fine editing continues

Fine cut approved

Soundtrack completed

Test showing to audiences

Original negative assembled

Advertising campaign approved

Prints of finished film

Formula films

Producers often reckon that what worked once will probably work again. Sometimes it does.

When a film is a success, there is always the temptation to make a 'follow-up' or sequel – or even to go back in time and screen events that might have happened before the story told in the first film (in which case the new film is known as a prequel). In 1976, a very successful film *Rocky*, told a rags-to-riches story of a boxer played by Sylvester Stallone. No less than four sequels were made to this film. *Star Wars*, *Star Trek* and *Superman* have been similarly exploited. Each set of films usually has the same main characters and follows the same formula. Hence a formula film is one which uses well-established plots and character types.

The term 'genre' describes a wider category: films that follow similar patterns and have similar character-types, or 'stock characters'. One genre, for example, is the Hollywood disaster movie, which always focuses on a terrifying calamity or emergency. *The Poseidon Adventure* was about a capsized liner, while *The Towering Inferno* was about a fire in the world's tallest building. There have been numerous aircraft disaster movies. Others, such as *Earthquake* and *Twister*, have featured natural disasters. Disaster movies often have unbelievable characters and dialogue but, for the film industry, they are a means of showing off newly developed special effects.

Audiences seem to like formula and genre films because they know what to expect. If you've seen one American gangster movie, liked it, and another is showing at your local

The James Bond films (made by United Artists) invariably offer similar mixtures of special effects, stunts, chases, guns, gadget-laden cars, explosions, sex and jokes. There are the regular characters (such as Q, M and Bond) and there is always a 'Bond Girl'.

Besides having different actors play Bond, United Artists have altered the genre in several ways. As the posters show, the 1997 film Tomorrow Never Dies *is very much more sophisticated than the first Bond film,* Dr No *(1962).*

cinema, you can expect to like that one too. Many of the most popular genres divide characters very clearly into goodies and baddies. They make complicated situations understandable, and the audience can feel comfortable because they know which side they are on, and the hero usually triumphs over evil. Because of this, **producers** and distributors like genre films too, as they are comparatively easy to sell.

Lazy film-makers who tackle a particular genre can end up making rather dull, repetitive films. But an inventive **director** can tweak, or vary, the format to make distinctive and memorable films.

Film genres can alter with the times. After America had fought the Vietnam War, there was a number of heroic war films which 're-fought' the war. Vietnam films then began to change. One film, *Platoon* (1986), raised the question of whether America should have fought the war at all.

Different genres have been popular at different times. In 1997, for example, there was a growing number of films with 'heroes-in-suits' – such as *Men in Black* and *Air Force One*.

Hammer Film Productions

This British company began making films in 1948, but only became really successful in the mid-50's when it began producing horror films. Two of its greatest box-office successes were *The Curse of Frankenstein* (1957) and *Dracula* (1958). There were several sequels. Typical features of the Hammer Horror Films were very vivid colour, a good deal of blood, and weak, victimized female characters.

Horror films allow us to feel the terror and fear we see on screen – but without real anxiety because we know subconsciously that the danger shown in the film cannot hurt us.

Westerns

The first western was *The Great Train Robbery*, which appeared in 1903. It introduced cinema-goers to the six-shooter, the train hold-up and the chase on horses – all to be seen in hundreds of future westerns. Stock western characters appeared regularly from then on: the lonesome wandering stranger on horseback, the black-hatted outlaw or villain, and the pretty female schoolteacher, for example. Other recurring elements included the scene in the drinking saloon, the chase and the final shoot-out. The typical western celebrated the untamed scenery of the American West, and the American ideals of independence and law and order. With their simple plots of good triumphing over evil, they had worldwide appeal. The American **studios** who made the films had no trouble exporting them around the world.

There were variations, such as the comic western, the introduction of the singing cowboy and, from 1950, westerns which sympathized with American Indians, traditionally portrayed as the 'baddies'.

But the genre seems to have had its day – perhaps because we now find it difficult to believe in 'simple' tales of good and evil; or perhaps because we are unhappy with stories which sideline women and exploit Native Americans. One of the best modern westerns (Kevin Costner's *Dances with Wolves*, 1990) paints a highly sympathetic picture of Native American culture.

The Hollywood system

Once the movie capital of the world, Hollywood was America's dream factory, with 50 studios producing hundreds of films a year.

Los Angeles, on the west coast of America, has a great climate. There are plenty of warm, bright days, even in winter. When the film industry began, few people lived there, and the land was cheap. Taxes were low. And nearby were miles and miles of spectacular and varied scenery: desert, mountains, seashore.... What more could a film-maker want? So, between 1910 and 1915, most American film companies moved from the east coast to LA – and in particular to one small suburb, Hollywood.

The movie moguls, or **studio** bosses (men such as Louis B. Mayer and Sam Goldwyn), had huge power. **Directors** and stars often had rude things to say about them, but it was the studio moguls who built up the film industry. As well as owning the studios, they each owned chains of cinemas across America in which they showed their own films. By the 1930s, Hollywood (and consequently the whole American film industry) was dominated by the seven biggest studios. They were Columbia, MGM, Paramount, RKO, Twentieth Century Fox, Universal and Warner Brothers. Between them they usually made over 500 films a year, and continued to be major producers of films up until the 1950s.

The star system

People have always gone to see films because of the actors they starred. Early film stars, such as Mary Pickford and Charlie Chaplin, attracted huge audiences. Chaplin moved from studio to studio, always demanding and getting more money. While that may have pleased him, the studios were unhappy. To prevent this happening in future, the studios began to employ young, unknown and much cheaper actors on long-term contracts. The studio then set about turning the actor into a star, through carefully managed publicity. For example, a young actress called Norma Jean Dougherty joined Twentieth Century Fox in the early 1950s. The studio turned her into Marilyn Monroe.

The star system saved the studios money, and gave young actors a good chance of success – but kept them tied to one studio. The star system also weakened the role of the director, who was often unable to choose the cast for his films.

Marilyn Monroe

The decline of the studios

A number of factors were responsible for the decline of the studio system:

• in 1948, the American Supreme Court ruled that film companies could no longer own cinemas
• television began to provide alternative entertainment
• more films were being made in Europe
• filming on location and abroad became cheaper.

Throughout the 1960s, Hollywood was in turmoil. In an attempt to compete with television, the studios produced huge, expensive epic films – many of which were failures.

Many studio bosses lost their jobs. Film companies were taken over by other companies. For example, Universal (along with Decca Records) was bought up by the Music Corporation of America (MCA). Columbia sold its own studio and moved in with Warner Brothers in 1972. That new organization was purchased by the Coca-Cola Company in 1982, and sold to the Sony Corporation of Japan in 1989.

Today, little is left of the old Hollywood system. Although film stars still live there, and many films are still shot there, most of the big movie companies have left or been bought up by even bigger international companies.

The majors

THE MAJOR PRODUCERS TODAY ARE: DISNEY; PARAMOUNT; WARNER BROTHERS; MCA/UNIVERSAL; TWENTIETH CENTURY FOX (KNOWN AS FOX); AND SONY PICTURES ENTERTAINMENT (WHICH INCLUDES COLUMBIA AND TRISTAR PICTURES).

MGM

METRO-GOLDWYN-MAYER WAS THE LARGEST AND MOST POWERFUL OF THE GREAT PRODUCTION COMPANIES, FROM ABOUT 1930 UNTIL AFTER WORLD WAR II. THE RISE OF TELEVISION, AND INCREASED PRODUCTION COSTS TOOK THEIR TOLL. MGM (NOW LINKED TO UNITED ARTISTS) RETURNED TO FILM PRODUCTION IN 1993.

Paramount Pictures Corporation

PARAMOUNT PICTURES BEGAN IN 1914. IT LED THE WAY IN DEVELOPING FILM SOUND AND BECAME FAMOUS FOR ITS COMIC FILMS (STARRING THE MARX BROTHERS, BOB HOPE AND OTHERS). ALTHOUGH IT PRODUCED A NUMBER OF FINANCIAL FLOPS, THE COMPANY HAS CONTINUED TO PRODUCE SOME HIGHLY SUCCESSFUL FILMS OVER THE YEARS, INCLUDING *SATURDAY NIGHT FEVER* (1977), *TOP GUN* (1986) AND *FORREST GUMP* (1994).

20th Century Fox

A MAJOR HOLLYWOOD STUDIO FORMED IN 1935, FOX BECAME FAMOUS FOR MAKING POPULAR MUSICALS. THE COMPANY FELL ON BAD TIMES WITH ITS EXPENSIVE AND DISASTROUS PRODUCTION OF *CLEOPATRA* IN 1963 (A $40-MILLION DUD), BUT *THE SOUND OF MUSIC* MADE THE STUDIO WEALTHY AGAIN IN 1965.

IN 1985 THE COMPANY WAS BOUGHT BY THE AUSTRALIAN MEDIA TYCOON RUPERT MURDOCH. DESPITE SUCCESSES LIKE *HOME ALONE* (1990) AND *MRS DOUBTFIRE* (1993), BY 1995 ITS EARNINGS HAD DROPPED TO 8% OF THE BOX-OFFICE MARKET.

The Walt Disney Company

WALT DISNEY BEGAN HIS CAREER IN 1919. SERIOUS SUCCESS CAME IN 1928, WHEN HIS COMPANY RELEASED *STEAMBOAT WILLIE*, A CARTOON INTRODUCING MICKEY MOUSE. THE COMPANY'S GOLDEN PERIOD SAW TWO FAMOUS FULL-LENGTH CARTOONS: *DUMBO* (1941) AND *BAMBI* (1942). IN RECENT YEARS, THE COMPANY HAS AGAIN HAD MUCH SUCCESS BY DEVELOPING COMPUTER ANIMATION – BUT IN 1997 IT MADE ONLY HALF THE NUMBER OF FILMS IT MADE IN 1996.

The British film industry

At times an Oscar-winning success story, but often a disaster area, the British film industry has had its ups and downs. Especially its downs.

Since 1896, when the first film was shown in London, films have been made in Britain. Many small production companies started up in those early days, but they failed to compete with imported films. Of the films shown in Britain in 1909, for example, only 15% were home-made, while 40% were French and 30% American. Five years later, 60% were American. By the end of 1924, no films were being made in Britain at all.

In 1927, the Government passed a law stating that a proportion of films shown in Britain must be British-made. As a result, American companies opened **studios** in Britain, making cheap films which became known as 'quota quickies'. Although many British films of this period were of a poor quality, some good **directors** did emerge. One was Alfred Hitchcock, later to be famous for his thrillers. Another was Alexander Korda, whose spectacular *The Private World of Henry VIII* (1933) was a success both in Britain and America. From then on, he faced a problem that still faces all British film-makers. Do you make risky, big-budget films that might or might not do well in America – or do you stick to smaller-scale films that will do well, but only in Britain?

The Rank Organisation

Headed by J Arthur Rank, this became the leading film company in England during the 1940s. At its peak, the company owned over half of England's studios and employed the country's best directors and performers. Besides production, it distributed films and owned its own chain of cinemas.

Carry On

In 1958, a production company called Anglo Amalgamated made a low-budget comedy called *Carry On Sergeant*. It was a surprise success, and the formula was used for a sequel, *Carry On Nurse*. This was Britain's highest-earning film of 1959.

30 *Carry On* films were made in all, the last being *Carry On Columbus* (1992). All were notable for their basic, rude humour. The best *Carry On* films made fun of other films: *Carry On Spying* (1964) parodied the Bond films, while *Carry On Screaming* (1966) mocked the Hammer Horror films. A perfect example of how successful a formula can be, they also prove to some people how unambitious British cinema has been at times.

Many successful comedies were made during the 1930s and 40s by Ealing Studios, when the Rank Organisation began to dominate the industry. During the 1940s, British cinema audiences reached their highest levels ever.

Film on Four

TEN OF CHANNEL 4'S
COMMISSIONS:

TRAINSPOTTING

A PRIVATE FUNCTION

LETTER TO BREZHNEV

MY BEAUTIFUL LAUNDERETTE

HOPE AND GLORY

FOUR WEDDINGS AND A FUNERAL

THE CRYING GAME

FEVER PITCH

PETER'S FRIENDS

THE MADNESS OF KING GEORGE

A scene from the early Channel 4 film My Beautiful Launderette.

With America showing new interest in investing in British films, and with new sources of funding for film-makers (such as the National Lottery), it has probably never been easier to get a **feature film** made in Britain. Certainly, there has been an extraordinary boom in production since the film and television industries began working together in the mid-80s.

Despite this growth, however, there is a problem which could bring the industry to its knees once again. British cinema chains often prefer to show lavish American films – so British film-makers can find it just as hard to get their films shown in British cinemas as to export them to America. With low or even no profits, small production companies have no money to invest in new films.

Some excellent (and successful) films were made, but decline set in during the 1950s with a predominance of low-budget comedies and cheap war and horror films. The 1960s saw a revival. Many new films with working-class heroes, and others which reflected life in the swinging sixties, became popular. This period is sometimes known as Britain's New Wave. Bad times returned during the 1970s, although some American blockbusters, such as the Bond films, *Star Wars* and *Batman*, were made in Britain.

By the early 1980s, things were looking disastrous. Producers, such as Rank and EMI, had various financial problems, and soon there were no major production companies at all. But a number of smaller, independent companies were springing up – thanks mainly to the start of the Channel 4 television station in 1982. It had a policy of encouraging film production, and commissioned a variety of new films for its *Film on Four* slot, which began in 1985. Channel 4 has become the biggest source of funding for British films, backing twelve to fifteen productions a year. Some it funds completely – to the tune of perhaps £1.5 million each. In the face of this competition, the BBC has set up its own film department, BBC Films, which has made some 80 films. Films like these are usually commissioned from independent film companies, such as Zenith.

UK film production

YEAR	TITLES PRODUCED	PRODUCTION COST (£M) (1997 PRICES)
1989	30	140.4
1990	60	262.9
1991	59	275.9
1992	47	201.7
1993	67	244.6
1994	84	486.2
1995	78	426.5
1996	128	759.2

Other film cultures

India, Japan and America have the biggest film industries in the world. But new industries have grown up in Mexico, Brazil and Australia.

India

India has a vast film industry. It produces more films than any other country in the world: approximately 900 each year. India of course has many languages (over 15 are officially recognized) and films are made in several of the most widely spoken ones. Calcutta is the centre of production for Bengali films, while films in Tamil tend to be made in Madras. The centre for Hindi language films is Bombay, which produces about one-quarter of India's movies. Because of this and because these films have the widest appeal, it is sometimes given the nickname Bollywood. Indeed, Bollywood films attract large audiences throughout Africa, the Middle East, China, the Far East and wherever people of Indian origin now live.

Indian films can be divided into two main types:
• Popular Cinema – Bombay has become famous for making the most popular 'all-India' films: films which, although they are in Hindi, overcome the barriers of language. Since sound was introduced in India in 1931, films have included much music and dancing. At times they have been accused of all being the same. Indeed, it has been said (unfairly) that every Indian film includes six songs, as many dances and hundreds of ways of showing men and women kissing without letting their lips touch. While many films certainly are conventional boy-meets-girl romances, the best **directors** have found ways of making original and different films out of this formula.

The leading actors are highly popular stars and are very well-paid. One who has had literally millions of fans is Amitabh Bachchan.

A Bollywood film poster.

More recent teenage heart-throbs include Salmaan Khan and Madhuri Dixit. Despite the importance of music in Indian popular films, the actors don't have to be great singers. Indian films are famous for their playback singers, who record the songs in advance for the actors to mime and dance to on the set. Indian audiences are quite aware of this and the playback singers have their own fans. One singer, Lata Mangeshkar, has made over 25,000 recordings.

• New or Parallel Cinema – India's 'New Cinema' began to flourish in the 1960s, thanks to government and private money. It is sometimes called 'Parallel Cinema' because it exists alongside, but is not connected to, popular or commercial cinema. It concentrates less on entertainment and more on showing India as it really is, and on addressing social concerns. One particularly famous film-maker, Satyajit Ray, won a major prize at the Cannes Film Festival in 1956. His films (such as the *Apu* trilogy, made in 1955–58) have become famous around the world, although his audience in India is limited.

European film production

THIS TABLE SHOWS THE LEADING FILM-PRODUCING COMPANIES WITHIN THE EUROPEAN COMMUNITY IN 1996.

COUNTRY	NO. OF FILMS (INCLUDING CO-PRODUCTIONS)	INVESTMENT ($MILLION)
DENMARK	21	39.20
FRANCE	134	634.70
GERMANY	63	258.60
IRELAND	18	83.90
ITALY	99	247.30
SPAIN	91	155.30
SWEDEN	31	71.00
UK	128	741.40

AS THIS TABLE SHOWS, THE COST OF AN INDIVIDUAL FILM VARIES CONSIDERABLY FROM COUNTRY TO COUNTRY.

Art House Cinemas

The Art House, or 'arts cinema', began to appear in the 1950s. The name refers to the type of smallish independent cinema that shows serious foreign-language and independent, non-commercial films. They appeal to film-goers who do not favour big popular cinemas and commercial films. In recent years, however, they have shown fewer foreign films because of decreasing numbers bought into UK distribution.

Japan

Before World War II, there were traditionally three types of Japanese films: warrior stories, love stories and stories about everyday life. They were cheaply made but, because they were shown in many Asian countries, they made a lot of money for their producers. Film production more or less stopped during the war. After the war, it recovered quickly. A key point came in 1951 when a Japanese film won first prize at the Venice Film Festival. In the next eighteen years, over 400 Japanese films won prizes at international film festivals, and Japan earned a reputation for quality films.

A famous Japanese film, made in 1954 by the film-maker Akira Kurosawa, was *The Seven Samurai*, about a medieval Japanese village attacked by bandits. The villagers find seven samurai or warriors to fight for them. In 1960, the American company United Artists made, *The Magnificent Seven*, a film set in Mexico telling almost exactly the same story, but with seven cowboys as the heroes.

A scene from The Seven Samurai.

Dubbing and subtitles

- A 'DUBBED VERSION' IS A FILM IN WHICH THE ORIGINAL DIALOGUE IS REPLACED BY A FOREIGN LANGUAGE VERSION. ALTHOUGH ATTEMPTS ARE USUALLY MADE TO MATCH THE NEW DIALOGUE TO THE MOVEMENTS OF THE LIPS OF THE CHARACTERS ON SCREEN, IT RARELY WORKS WELL.
- ALTERNATIVELY, SUBTITLES CAN BE SUPERIMPOSED AT THE BOTTOM OF THE PICTURE, ALLOWING THE AUDIENCE TO READ A TRANSLATION OF THE ORIGINAL DIALOGUE.
- IN THE PAST, TWO VERSIONS WERE SOMETIMES MADE OF A FILM — USING DIFFERENT ACTORS SPEAKING DIFFERENT LANGUAGES. THIS IS RARELY DONE NOW, BECAUSE OF THE HIGH COST.

Distribution

The distributor doesn't just deliver a copy of the film to each cinema. The distributor makes sure a film makes money. Or that's the theory.

As soon as a film goes into production, the business of marketing and selling it to cinemas and to the public must get underway. This process, as well as actually sending out copies of the films for showing, is called distribution. The people or companies that perform these tasks are called distributors. Distributors are either huge multinational companies or small independent companies. In either case, they all follow certain stages in the process of distribution.

The distributor buys the rights to a film in one or more countries. 'The rights' means the authority to hire copies to cinemas, and to publicize the film. A **producer** and distributor often sign an agreement for seven years. The payment for the rights may be made before the start of the film's production, or after it has been completed.

The distribution process includes:
• arranging for the manufacture of enough copies of the film
• designing, producing and distributing advertising and publicity material, and trying

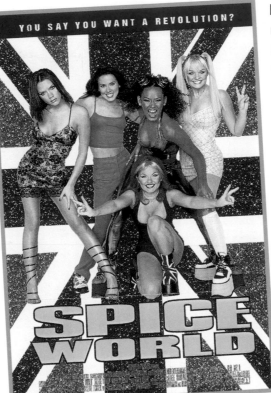

A precisely organized publicity campaign helped launch this £15 million film.

to get newspapers, radio and television interested in the film – because the more a film is written and talked about before it is first shown, the more chance it has of being a success
• sending out copies of the film and advertising matter to each cinema that has booked it
• organizing any merchandizing deals – for example, selling licences to make T-shirts, CDs, toys, board games, etc.

For the release of potential blockbuster films, major distributors may require up to 100% of the box-office takings as a rental fee for the first week. After that, the distributor will take diminishing percentages for each succeeding week. Such percentages are calculated after the cinema's fixed expenses (such as wages) have been subtracted. The money the cinema subtracts is known as 'the house nut'.

The release date
Once they have seen a film, distributors plan its release date (its first showing) very carefully. Schedules for the key periods of the summer holidays and Christmas are planned eight months in advance.

Usually a firm release date is set for London's West End, then slightly later dates are arranged for 'the key cities'. These include Birmingham, Brighton, Bristol, Cardiff, Edinburgh, Glasgow, Leeds, Manchester, Newcastle and Sheffield. If a distributor is not sure whether a film will be a success, it might be tried out in London and one key city, before going on **general release**.

Typically, a film is shown for about six months in different cinemas, then spends a similar period available for video rental. It can then go into what is called the sell-through market, where consumers can buy the video outright.

After this, it becomes available for showing on television. The Sky Television (BSkyB) movie channels (available on satellite and by cable) screen most films between twelve and eighteen months after first release. The ordinary, non-satellite channels (BBC

Television, ITV and Channels 4 and 5) don't usually get their hands on a film until two years after its release date.

Digital satellite television brings the possibility of video on demand. The operators of these services can offer 'pay-per-view'(PPV) films screened simultaneously on multiple channels at fifteen-minute intervals. This means that if satellite subscribers are prepared to pay extra to watch a particular film, they can watch it whenever they want to, because it will be starting on one of the digital channels every fifteen minutes.

The UK distributors

In Britain, five distributors market the output of the US Major **studios**. The largest, United International Pictures (UIP), is the distributor for MGM, Paramount and Universal. In 1996, typically, it dominated the British cinema scene with 29 films, which took nearly £95 million at the box office.

The others distribute varying numbers of films each year. In 1996, the five 'US Major' distributors released the following numbers of American films:

UIP	29
Buena Vista	26
Warner	20
20th Century Fox	16
Columbia	13

The number of films distributed is not a guide to success. Warner, for example, earned less in 1996 than Fox or Columbia.

There are also about 160 independent distributors in Britain who distribute films from sources other than the US Major producers. Some of these, such as Polygram, have links with European companies. Among the larger and more successful are Entertainment, Polygram, Artificial Eye, Pathé and Film Four.

DID YOU KNOW?•FACTS & FIGURES•INDUSTRY STATI

The Oscars

THE OSCARS ARE GOLD-PLATED STATUETTES AWARDED EVERY MARCH OR APRIL BY THE ACADEMY OF MOTION PICTURE ARTS AND SCIENCES, FOR THE BEST ACHIEVEMENTS IN PERFORMANCE AND FILMMAKING DURING THE PREVIOUS CALENDAR YEAR. THE CEREMONY INCLUDES CATEGORIES SUCH AS BEST FILM, BEST ACTOR, BEST ACTRESS, BEST SCREENPLAY, BEST DIRECTING, AND SO ON. THE FIGURINES ARE SUPPOSEDLY NICKNAMED OSCARS BECAUSE A LIBRARIAN WHO ONCE WORKED AT THE ACADEMY SAID THEY LOOKED LIKE HER UNCLE OSCAR. THE PUBLICITY CREATED BY THE AWARDS HELPS TO SELL THE WINNING FILMS.

The Oscar statuette awarded to Juliette Binoche for her role in The English Patient.

Exhibition

Popcorn, posters and cake stands – there's more to managing a cinema than putting a film in a projector.

During the 1930s, cinema-going was an increasingly popular activity. Grand new picture palaces were built – some of the grandest being the Odeon cinemas. They had only one auditorium (seating area) each, but the largest could seat at least 1,000 people. Many of these older cinemas have now been converted to include three or four auditoriums. Others were converted into bowling alleys, bingo halls or skating rinks. The number of cinema tickets sold each year has dramatically fallen since the 1930s and 40s.

Up until about 1960, cinema-goers expected a double feature programme. This included one or two cartoons and a newsreel (a round-up of the previous week's news stories), as well as two **feature films**. The major film was known as the A-picture. B-pictures had smaller budgets and less famous stars.

Nowadays there is cut-throat competition between the cinema companies that own the cinemas to book the best films. By the time a film is first shown at a film festival, a cinema circuit such as ABC or Odeon may already have bought it up. The main circuits in 1996 were:

	Cinema sites	Screens
ABC	92	244
Odeon	73	362
UCI	26	232
Virgin	24	162
Warner Village	16	143
Showcase	14	181
Independent cinemas	437	679

A strong light inside a projector beams the filmed picture outwards and onto the screen.

Projection

The film is beamed onto the cinema screen from the projection room. The actual films are kept on reels and each reel holds about twenty minutes – so a typical film might need five or six reels. The projection room also contains the controls for playing music, operating the curtains and dimming the lights.

For many years, at least two projectors were needed to show a film. The first reel was shown on Projector No 1, while the second reel was made ready on the second projector. As the first reel ended, the projectionist switched to Projector No 2 so that the film carried on without a break. Reel No 3 could then be put onto the first projector. In practice, it was usually fairly easy to tell when the jump between projectors happened.

Today, the reels are more often joined together and placed on what is known as a cake stand or platter.

A modern 'cake stand' projector loader.

Mini, Multi and Mega

The number of cinemas with more than one screen or auditorium has gradually increased. This is because not enough people now want to see the same film at the same time to make it worth showing it in a large cinema. There are now several types of multi-screen cinema:

- miniplex: cinema with up to six screens
- multiplex: cinema with up to twelve screens
- megaplex: cinema with up to 32 screens.

The spread of the multi-screen cinema does not mean more cinema seats. In America the number of cinema screens grew from 17,590 in 1980 to 27,805 in 1995. In the same period, however, the actual number of seats decreased.

The film travels from this to the projector itself and, just as it does in the camera (see page 11), stops for a brief moment in the **gate**. A shutter opens and the **frame**, or picture, is projected through the lens onto the screen. As the film leaves the gate, it passes the soundtrack reader. A light shines onto the soundtrack, picks up the information stored in the soundtrack and carries it to a photoelectric cell that transmits the sound to the loudspeakers.

Projection is becoming more automated. An entire performance of over four hours can come off a single cake stand or platter. It is fed back from the projector onto a second platter in such a way that the film need not be rewound. Cues placed on the film automatically perform jobs such as operating the curtains, lights and music.

UK box office 1996

ADMISSIONS	£123.8 MILLION
BOX OFFICE GROSS	£426 MILLION
AVERAGE TICKET PRICE	£3.44

UK cinemas and screens

YEAR	TOTAL CINEMA SITES	TOTAL SCREENS
1986	660	1,249
1991	724	1,789
1996	742	2,166

OF THE 742 CINEMAS OPEN IN 1996, 95 WERE MULTIPLEXES. THESE 95 HAD 859 SCREENS.

Frequency of cinema-going in 1996

AGE GROUP	7-14	15-24	25-34	35+
% WHO GO ONCE A MONTH	15%	22%	12%	5%
% WHO GO TO THE CINEMA	95%	94%	88%	58%

Television and video

Television and cinema were once deadly enemies, with television feeding off the cinema. Television profits now pay for films.

During the 1960s, television began to be a serious rival to the cinema. By 1984, cinema attendance was at an all-time low. This didn't mean people weren't watching films: they were just waiting to see them on television. In that year, it was estimated that audiences for cinema films on television were 2.4 times as large as cinema audiences themselves. What is more, television was obtaining the rights to show films at comparatively low prices.

Television had also started to make its own films, designed to be shown just on television, in 1964. These became known as 'made-for-television' films. Then, in the mid-1980s, television companies began making films that were also suitable for showing in cinemas. That is, they were made on 35mm film, on a widescreen **aspect ratio**, and with stereo sound (then quite rare in television programme making). The leader in this field was Channel 4 (see page 19). These films had to have a cinema release before being shown on television – otherwise nobody would pay to see them. This was one reason the BBC was slow to start making films for cinema release. Since the BBC is funded by television licence payers, it was thought that the viewers should have the first chance to see any BBC productions.

Made-for-TV films

Films made for showing only on television can be shorter than films made for the cinema. They can also have several episodes, and can offer a more in-depth treatment of a story than the normal two-hour cinema film. Not all drama made for television is made on film – some is taped on video.

The film and television industries have not only become entwined in terms of production. The film industry relies heavily on income from television and video exhibition of its productions. Indeed, it has been estimated that, in 1997, three times as many people now watch home videos as go to the cinema, so much of the film industry's profits for a film comes from video rentals and sales – and, increasingly, from subscription and pay-per-view television channels.

UK-consumer spending on feature films

Year	Box Office (£M)	Video Rental (£M)	Video Retail (£M)	Movie Channel Subscription (£M)	Total (£M)
1986	142	375	70	-	587
1991	295	540	444	121	1,400
1996	426	491	803	1,319	3,039

ACTION FILMS LIKE BAD BOYS AND WATERWORLD DO WELL IN THE VIDEO RENTAL MARKET. IN THE VIDEO RETAIL MARKET FAMILY FILMS DO BETTER – FILMS SUCH AS TOY STORY, 101 DALMATIANS AND BABE. AS DIGITAL TELEVISION BECOMES WIDESPREAD, THE VIDEO RENTAL MARKET MAY COLLAPSE.

BSkyB

The satellite television network BSkyB has signed deals which allow it the right to the first television exhibition (on pay TV) of films from Columbia, Disney, MGM, Paramount, 20th Century Fox, and Universal…. Consequently virtually all Hollywood's top box office films get to be shown on the BSkyB Movie Channels.

Box office

Even though a considerable portion of a film's earnings come from video and television exhibition, the box office is still a key factor. How well a film does in the cinema can make or break its reputation. However, few films cover their cost at the box office. Most films usually only break even (earn back all their costs) when their **gross** earnings are taken into account. As well as income from the box office, gross earnings include profits from spin-offs, such as video and television earnings, and sales of toys, clothes, games, etc. linked to the film.

In Britain, the cinemas showing the film get their share of the takings first. VAT must be paid on the film's gross take. Then the distributors get their costs and profits back. After that, the film-makers must pay off all the production costs. Only then do the **producers** stand a chance of making any profit – out of which they might finance a new film. In Britain, a film can be a success for the exhibitor and distributor, while the producer loses money.

Videotape

Although the picture quality of videotape has improved remarkably, its images still lack the brightness, contrast, colour and immediacy of images filmed. The video of a film never looks as good as the film does in the cinema.

However, video is making important inroads in the **editing** of film. The editor of a film may first transfer it to videotape and then do the editing electronically, trying out different arrangements until he or she is satisfied with the sequence. It is much quicker to try out different 'cuts' on video than on film. Once a sequence has been decided, the editor then returns to edit the actual film.

Digital effects

Special-effects filming is developing rapidly, thanks to computer technology. One early leader in this area was George Lucas, **director** of the *Star Wars* films.

Images from a film or drawing are electronically scanned into a computer, where they are stored digitally. In effect, they become video pictures on the monitor. They can then be made to move or change in various ways.

The film Toy Story (1995) did not use puppets or models. The characters and scenery were never real, but were created digitally in a computer.

Sex, violence and censorship

If a film includes a scene which might encourage just one person to go out and commit a violent crime, should that scene be censored?

The cinema has been censored since its earliest days. In America the National Board of Censors began work in 1909 while in Britain the British Board of Film Censors, or BBFC, was established in 1912. In its early days the BBFC had only two rules: there should be no nudity; and the character of Jesus Christ should never be portrayed in a film. By the 1930s, it had 98 rules. Among other things, these rules prevented anything topical or controversial being shown in a **feature film**. In 1937, its president, Lord Tyrell boasted: 'We may take pride in observing that there is not a single film showing in London today which deals with any of the burning issues of the day.'

In 1985, the BBFC became the **British Board of Film Classification** (**BBFC**).

The Hays Code

In 1922 the American National Board of Censors was replaced by the Motion Picture Producers and Distributors of America (MPPDA). The MPPDA and its president, Will H. Hays, put considerable pressure on the **studios** to control the sexual content of their films. In 1930, the 'Hays Code' laid down rules about what could be shown.

In general, films were not to be explicitly sexual or violent, they were not to condone crime, and irreverent references to religion – even common swear words were to be avoided. In 1939, the **producer** of the film *Gone with the Wind* was fined $5,000 for allowing the famous line, 'Frankly my dear, I don't give a damn.' In 1952, however, the American Supreme Court freed films from censorship on religious grounds, and the collapse of the code began.

*In 1971, the **director** Stanley Kubrick made a film of a novel by Anthony Burgess called* A Clockwork Orange, *in which a young man becomes increasingly addicted to violence. It was blamed for starting a cult of aggression. Both Kubrick and Burgess came to believe that the film did encourage a particular way of being violent, and since 1973 it has been withdrawn from exhibition in Britain – at Kubrick's request.*

Feature films on TV

The Independent Television Commission (which supervises ITV, Channel 4 and Channel 5, as well as the satellite and cable channels) has its own rules about the scheduling of feature films on television:

- no 12-rated version should normally start before 8 pm on any service
- no 15-rated version should normally start before 9 pm (or 8 pm on premium rate subscription channels)
- no 18-rated version should start before 10 pm on any service
- no R18-rated version should be transmitted at any time
- no version which has been refused a BBFC certification should be transmitted at any time.

The debate continues

The debate about censorship or control of what is shown in films continues. Experts cannot agree whether violent films encourage some people to be violent themselves. If a woman is treated brutally in a film, does that lead some viewers to think it is all right to treat women in that way? If a character gets away with drunken driving, can that lead to copycat behaviour? If smoking appears glamorous or smart, does that encourage people to smoke? Have we relaxed the rules too much?

Or should **producers** be allowed to show what they like in a film – and should we be allowed to see what we want on the screen?

Film classifications

Since 1913, the BBFC has viewed every film, and no film can be shown in public in Britain without a BBFC certificate. When viewing a film, the BBFC considers first if the film breaks any law, for example by 'depraving and corrupting' people. It then considers if the film contains anything that might be 'greatly ... offensive to a large number of people' and then decides on which certificate the film should have. Since 1989, there have been the following categories of certificate:

 Universal: the film can be seen by people of all ages.

Parental Guidance: parents might wish to check the film before showing it to young children. There might be some violence, some sex scenes or brief nudity. It might also contain some mild swear words.

  Films with these classification symbols are deemed unsuitable for anyone younger than these ages.
R18: For Restricted Distribution in premises to which no under-18s are admitted.

Local authorities, who grant licences to cinemas, can still ban a film even when the BBFC has given it a certificate. They can also alter the category of a certificate. Since 1985, the BBFC has also issued certificates for videos. Videos of feature films usually, but not always, get the same category certificate as the cinema version. There is one additional video category, Uc, which means that the film has a Universal category and is suitable for everyone – especially young children.

Key dates

1889	Friese-Greene, an Englishman, patents the first real cinematograph machine.
1892	Edison develops the Kinetograph camera, which uses sprocket holes.
1896	Two French brothers called Lumière give the first public showing of moving pictures of real life.
1900	A 'talking' movie, made using a gramophone record and silent film, is shown in Paris.
1902	First special effects used in a French film about space travel.
1908	First colour films are made.
1910	*In Old California* is the first film to be made in Hollywood.
1912	Chronophone system is developed, using audio discs linked to accompanying silent films.
1913	British Board of Film Censors applies its first rules.
1914	The first movie palace, the Strand, opens in New York City – seating an audience of nearly 3,000.
1920s	Development of artificial lighting and colour photography.
1926	Warner Brothers launch their Vitaphone sound system (also using audio discs to store the sound).
1927	Cinematograph Act is passed in Britain.
	The Jazz Singer is the first 'talkie'.
1928	First video disc.
	Full-colour home movies are now possible, using 16 mm film.
	First all-colour, all-talking musical, *On with the Show*.
1929	First in-flight movie is shown on an aircraft.
	First Oscars are awarded.
1931	A law is passed in Britain making it legal to show films on Sundays.
1933	British Film Institute is founded 'to promote the appreciation, enjoyment, protection and development of moving image culture'.
1936	192 films are produced in Britain – the most in any one year.
	Pinewood **studios** open.
1939	Hollywood studios are producing 500 films a year.
1940	Walt Disney's *Fantasia* uses a stereophonic system.
1946	Cinema attendances in Britain reach their highest-ever figure: 1,635,000,000.
	First Cannes Film Festival (important international festival held annually in the South of France).
1952	**Cinerama** is launched.
1953	**CinemaScope** is launched by Twentieth Century Fox.
1955	Disneyland opens.
1957	Cinema attendance in Britain falls to 915,200,000 (the lowest figure since 1934).
1962	First James Bond film, *Dr No*, opens.
	Death of Walt Disney.
1965	*The Sound of Music* achieves the highest **gross** income of any film to date.
1971	National Film School opens.
1977	**Dolby** stereo sound is introduced.
	Charlie Chaplin dies.
	Star Wars opens.
1980	Alfred Hitchcock dies.
1981	Only 24 films are produced in Britain.
1982	Channel 4 begins.
1984	Cinema attendance in Britain reaches its lowest-ever figure: 54,000,000.
1985	Channel 4 begins commissioning films for cinema release. BBFC becomes **British Board of Film Classification**.
1990	Sky Movies becomes Britain's first pay-per-view satellite channel.
1995	The number of cinema screens in Britain grows to 2,166.
1997	Cinema admissions rise to 139 million, the highest since 1974.

Glossary

aspect ratio   relationship between the width and height of a film **frame** or a picture on the screen. The standard picture ratio is 1.33:1 (4 units long by 3 units high), whereas most modern 35mm films in Britain are made in the much wider Standard European Wide Screen format of 1.66:1 (5 units long by 3 units high).

British Board of Film Classification (BBFC)   organization that issues certificates to films and videos (see pages 28–29)

call sheet   printed pages of instructions for the following day's filming, telling everyone involved exactly which scenes will be shot and when and where to turn up

celluloid   type of plastic used to make camera film

CinemaScope   widescreen film image

Cinerama   widescreen process using three projectors to produce one image onto a curved screen

clapper/loader   member of the camera crew in charge of loading and unloading film from the camera, and marking the beginning and end of each **take** with the clapperboard (see page 10)

credits   names and jobs of those involved in making a film

cutting room   room where **editing** is done

director   person in charge of directing the action of a film and then **editing** it

dissolve   technique that makes one film image fade into another one

Dolby   system in sound recording that helps cut out background noise and distortion

dubbing or **post-sync**   re-recording dialogue in a sound studio after the film has completed shooting, to improve sound quality

editing   process of cutting down and re-arranging recorded material

exterior   scene that takes place out of doors

extras   non-speaking actors who act as crowds, villagers, soldiers, etc.

feature film   full-length film, usually fictional e.g. recounting a story

film stock   unused rolls of **celluloid** film

first assistant director   director's right-hand person, (see page 10)

first run   first showing of a film, usually (in Britain) in selected London cinemas

focus   control on a camera which, by moving the **lens**, allows the operator to film the main subject without any blurring

focus puller   camera operator's assistant who adjusts the **focus** of the lens during filming

footage   length of exposed film

frame   one complete picture on a piece of film

gaffer   chief electrician on a film, in overall charge of the lights

gate   part of a camera or projector in front of the **lens**, through which the film passes

gauge   size or width of film, such as 35mm or 16mm

general release   exhibition (showing) of a film in cinemas across the country

gofer, gopher   person who goes on errands and odd jobs during production (so-called because they 'go for' things)

gross   total revenue of a film, from both box office and spin-offs

interior   scene filmed inside a studio **set** or inside a building

in the can   after shooting, film is kept in a strong canister, on its way to and from the lab; so when a scene is 'in the can' this means it has been shot

lens   disc of glass or plastic, thicker in the middle than at the edges. It bends beams of light to control how a camera 'sees'.

panning   movement of the camera to the left or right, often in order to shoot the full breadth of a scene

post-sync   see **dubbing**

producer   person in overall charge of the finance, control and planning of a film (see pages 4-9)

reaction shot   shot showing a character's response to a piece of action or dialogue

reverse shot   shot taken from the opposite direction to the previous one (used when two characters are talking)

rushes   developed sections of film returned from the lab and ready to be viewed

set   room or building built to film any one particular scene, or the area used for a scene outside

shooting script   final version of the script, and the one used for the filming

storyboard   series of sketches showing the key scenes of the material to be shot

studio   specially-built, sound-proofed building where **interior** scenes are shot

take   one version of a particular shot or scene being filmed. There can be many takes of the same scene.

treatment   preliminary script showing how a film or programme might be put together (see page 5)

unit   whole film crew

wrap   end of filming at the end of the day, or when filming is completed on the whole film

Index